Road Trip Games

& Activities

FOR KIDS

33 original and classic games
for back seat fun

CATHERINE RYAN GREGORY

TRAVEL TIPS FOR REAL FAMILIES

ToAndFroFam.com

Copyright © 2020 Catherine Ryan Gregory

Book Resources

Free printables that accompany some activities in this book can be downloaded at ToAndFroFam.com/games.

Become a family travel pro by learning smart strategies and systems via ToandFroFam.com/courses.

Dedication

To Eric, my partner and forever person.
I'm so lucky we're on this adventure together.

Contents

Introduction

We were about a hundred miles into a six-hour road trip. As we hurtled down the highway at 65 miles an hour, my kids grew restless. Then Edie, my older daughter, asked the dreaded question that keeps families at home instead of traveling together:

"Are we there yet?"

I knew I had to act fast before I had a back seat mutiny on my hands. So I did what generations of parents before me have done: I suggested we play a road trip game.

Soon enough, it was my younger daughter Maxine's turn. "I spy with my little eye something that is… pink!" she announced.

Outside, miles and miles of brown hills stretched into the distance. I saw different shades of beige but, alas, no pink. Finally, we all gave up.

"It's a flamingo swimming pool!" she squealed, clearly pleased that she stumped us all.

Where, exactly, was that pink flamingo swimming pool? Far, far away behind the mountains, Maxine explained.

Ah. Of course.

Making memories as a family

Max will never, ever live down the notorious flamingo swimming pool incident—and that's one of the most beautiful things about engaging with your kiddos on a road trip. We'll laugh about this game, and many others, for years to come.

That's what happens when you and your kids match wits, guess each other's mystery item or collaborate on a wacky storytelling challenge: You make memories together.

These days, families are stretched thin. I'm pretty sure you can empathize. Whether it's a crammed calendar full of extracurricular activities or simply trying to balance your kids' online school with your newly remote job, there's less time today to simply *have fun together*.

Add in screens and you may feel like you hardly see your littles anymore.

I totally get this. I work for myself and am always balancing at least four gigs. Meanwhile, my kids are both doing online school with my stay-at-home-dad husband. Whenever we have some down time, I want to zone in on my kids, who I know will be this little once and only once.

Yet competing distractions vie for my attention. The *shoulds* pile up: I should wipe out the fridge. We should get dinner started. I should help Edie get caught up in her distance learning curriculum. I should finally make Maxine wash her hair in the bath.

Should. Should. Should.

That's why I'm such a cheerleader for family travel: You literally get away from it all.

Reviving the road trip

As the world changes, families are taking more road trips together than ever. You might have planned more road trips recently to avoid flying, to trim your travel budget or to create the kind of undistracted time together you crave.

You'd be in good company. In summer 2020 alone, people in the U.S. took an estimated *683 million* road trips. And a full 70% of parents say they have a great time on those car-based vacations.

I'm not surprised. Hitting the road as a family is one of the best ways to block out distractions and simply *be together*.

That said, if you're like most parents, you feel at least a tad apprehensive about piling into the car with your crew. No matter how many miles there are between A and B, you'll need something to do to pass the time.

(And *Paw Patrol* DVDs on repeat are probably not what you had in mind.)

That's where this games guide comes in.

Hours of fun together

In the following pages, you'll find 33 games and activities hand-picked for family road trips. You'll recognize the classics *and* learn some new ones. Your family is almost sure to pick a fresh favorite—or *favorites*!

I'm a busy parent like you, so I know you don't have time to scour the internet for how-to instructions or download a million different printables from Pinterest. That's why I collected these fun activities in one place.

Flip through the options, pick a game at random or methodically work through the entire games guide: How you use **Road Trip Games & Activities for Kids** is up to you!

Each game is also customizable. Find suggestions to make an activity harder or easier, depending on the ages and stages of your kids. That way, the whole family—from toddlers to teens—has fun en route!

Embrace the journey

When Edie asked that question on the "flamingo swimming pool road trip"—you know the one, "Are we there yet?"—I should have said *yes*. We were hours from our destination, but we were just where we should be: together.

Road trips aren't about speeding from here to there as quickly as you can. They're as much about the time together in the car as they are about wherever you're driving to.

I know you'll make the most of those moments. Road Trip Games & Activities for Kids will help.

So fill up the tank and buckle up: You're about to rev up the fun on your best family road trip yet.

Safety note

The following 33 games are meant for fun, of course. But fun never, ever trumps safety.

I trust that you will always keep safety top of mind whenever you're on the road, including when you're playing games. I've noted a number of activities that can include the driver (look for the Driver-safe category).

That said, use your best judgment. There may be times when the driver needs to focus 100% of their attention on the road and any game play would be distracting. You may also find safe ways to adapt games not marked Driver-safe so that everyone in the car can play.

To wrap this up, it is critical—for you, your family and everyone else on the road—that safety is always your top priority.

Category Key

Throughout the book, you'll see icons at the top of each entry. These icons identify the subjects covered in each activity.

Competition

Driver-Safe

Guessing

Memory

Road Trip Games & Activities for Kids

Music

Numbers

Out the Window

Printable

Teamwork

Word Games

33 GAMES & ACTIVITIES FOR ROAD TRIP FUN

1
Is It Bigger Than
a Breadbox?

Categories:

- Guessing

This is my all-time favorite family road trip game. I grew up playing it with my parents and siblings as we drove to the Oregon Coast or to Idaho for a week-long kayaking trip. My younger sister will never, ever live down the time she stumped the entire carful of us when she chose the household item of *dust*.

Seriously.

Whether or not you allow dust to qualify as a household item, you and your kids will get a kick out of this game. Anyone can play it because you don't need an understanding of math, the alphabet or anything else, really. Give it a go and see if you agree that it's, well, pretty much the best thing since sliced you-know-what.

Directions

The goal of the game is to guess which household object someone is thinking of.

The person who begins the game thinks of an item often found inside the home. The rest of the passengers take turns asking yes or no questions. The first question of the game is always, "Is it bigger than a breadbox?" (In case you didn't grow up with a breadbox, it's the size of a loaf of bread, understandably.)

As the game progresses, the questions passengers ask ("Is it commonly found in the kitchen?" "Is it made of metal?" "Do we have one?") will help them narrow down the many, many possible household objects. The game is finished when someone correctly guesses that round's item.

Continue the game by having someone new think up an object.

Note: If your family loves to find every game's loopholes, establish some rules ahead of the game.

For example, you might explain that it's fine to choose "toy" as a household object, but "my lovey bunny Louise" is too specific.

Make it easier

Make Is It Bigger Than a Breadbox easier by limiting the kinds of items you can think of. You can come up with household objects that are found in the bathroom, for example, or ones that the whole family uses. This is helpful so a young sibling doesn't feel left out when Big Brother thinks of "corkscrew," something little kids are unlikely to know.

Make it harder

When you're up for playing multiple rounds, announce that every passenger will have three opportunities to think up an item. The twist: All three items will be related in some way. The game's final challenge is for all the other passengers to figure out what the common theme is.

For example, if someone came up with dog bowl, toilet and door mat, the connecting theme could be "things that get dirty and need to be cleaned." The items remote control, cell phone charger and keys could be connected by the theme "things Dad loses all the time."

Fun Facts

Germans eat the most bread of anyone in the world.

The average American home contains 300,000 items.

2
Fortunately/Unfortunately

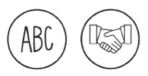

Categories:

- Word games
- Teamwork

You might remember the extreme mood swings your kids experienced when they were toddlers... or teenagers. (If you're in the midst of that phase now, I'm sending you solidarity.) No matter your kids' ages and stages, they'll have fun putting a story's character through dramatic ups and downs.

Fortunately/Unfortunately is sure to get everyone to laugh. In fact, it's the perfect game for when things *aren't* going smoothly on your road trip. You can even incorporate your own trip's bumps in the road into the game.

For example, if you drive through a major city during rush hour, incorporate that scenario into the Fortunately/Unfortunately story. That could look like: "Unfortunately, the Gregory family road trip came to a standstill on the I-90. Fortunately, their minivan doubled as a rocket and could fly over the traffic."

See what wacky scenarios your family can come up with next.

Directions

One person starts the game with a sentence that begins the story. It could be something as mundane as "One day, my dog barked at the garbage truck" or as extraordinary as "Earlier this morning, I became a mermaid."

The next person adds to the story with a sentence that begins, "Unfortunately…" It will contain a scenario that turns the story for the worst!

The next person continues the story with a sentence that begins, "Fortunately…" and somehow reverses the bad luck of the previous sentence.

The game continues in this pattern for as long as passengers want to. Anyone can stop the game by announcing "The End" on their turn.

Make it easier

If your kids are having a hard time with the fortunately/unfortunately vocabulary, you can make it easier to grasp by using good news/bad news instead. For example, they could say, "Good news: The avalanche was made of ice cream! Bad news: I didn't have a spoon."

Make it harder

To make this open-ended storytelling game harder, it can't end until it comes full circle. That is, the story has to come back to its beginning.

So if the story started with a pirate leaving port on his first-ever raiding voyage, the story—and game—won't end until the pirate arrives back at that original port.

Fun Facts

The ups and downs of the story you create can feel like a zigzag motion, right? In the United Kingdom, zigzags actually prevent accidents! Zigzags are painted onto the street in the U.K. to warn drivers of an upcoming crosswalk so they know to slow down and look out for pedestrians.

3
Body Part Dance Party

Categories:

- Music

My mom may or may not have invented this wacky activity at my kitchen table. One day she told my kids about a game in which you take turns dancing with only a single part of your body. They loved it so much that some days, they suggest we play it at every meal.

The good thing about throwing a Body Part Dance Party is that you can do it in the car. You don't need to waltz across a room or swing yer partner 'round and 'round, and you definitely don't have the space to do that in your ride anyway!

Instead, turn on some tunes and rock out—with your pinky finger, elbow or nostril!

Directions

Cue up some fun, danceable music the whole family will like. Push play.

Each passenger takes turns picking the body part to dance with. They shout, "[Body part] dance party!" (e.g. "Eyebrows dance party!"). Everyone in the car—minus the driver, if that's unsafe—boogies down with only that body part.

Dance for a bit, until the following person shouts out the next dance party.

Make it easier

Body Part Dance Parties aren't competitive or hard, but you can do a few variations. One person can be the DJ, changing the song whenever it's time for a new body part dance.

You can also make a Body Part Dance Party playlist ahead of time. Choose songs that refer to parts of the body (e.g. "Brown Eyed Girl" and "Footloose").

Make it harder

Take turns making up a signature body part dance move. Everyone else in the car has to mimic it! Will anyone else do the shoulder shimmy as well as you do? Will you match your kiddo's eyebrow wiggle? Time for a body part dance-off.

Fun Facts

The human body contains more than 600 muscles. Some of them you control (like your abdominals when you shake your hips); others work without you thinking about them (like your stomach when you digest lunch).

Fandango is a dance from Spain. The word also means foolishness.

4
Road Trip Bingo

Categories:

- Printable
- Out the window

Directions

Before you leave home, print out the Road Trip Bingo printables, which you can download for free at ToAndFroFam.com/games. You can also make your own by writing, drawing or pasting clip art of road trip-related items into a 5x5 grid. (If you DIY, incorporate location-specific items into the card, like a saguaro cactus if you're taking a road trip through the Southwest USA.)

Hand the Bingo boards to your kids. They'll have an easier time if they rest the board on a clipboard or sturdy book.

They'll look out the window and mark off the items they see on their board. They can cover the square with a sticker, cross it off with marker or stick a magnet on it if you have a metal tray to place the board on.

You can play regular Bingo (5 squares in a row), 4 corners, X (with diagonal lines running left to right and right to left) or blackout.

Make it easier

If your kiddos like Road Trip Bingo as much as mine do, and you don't want to print off a million copies, slide the boards into a plastic sheet protector. Kids can then use a dry erase pen to mark off the squares they've found. Simply wipe it clean when the game is done, and it's ready to play again later.

Make it harder

Give the winner of Road Trip Bingo more than bragging rights. The first person to get a Bingo, four corners or blackout wins something fun, like rights to DJ the music for an hour or the choice of where to stop for lunch.

Fun Facts

"Bingo" used to be called "Beano" because players covered their squares with dry beans.

There are more Bingo winners called Margaret than any other name.

5
Alphabet out the Window

Categories:

- Word games
- Printable
- Out the window

Whether your kids are working on learning their ABCs or are much older and expanding vocab for their SATs, this game gives them a chance to practice in the car.

Alphabet out the Window is also wonderfully open-ended. That means you can play it multiple times over the course of your road trip. And since the scenery is always changing, you'll never play the same game twice!

Directions

Before you leave home, print and cut out the Alphabet Out The Window ABCs cards, found at ToAndFroFam.com/games. I recommend punching a hole in the corner of each card and storing them on a binder ring. (That way you don't lose letters!) You can also make your own alphabet set by writing each letter on a small piece of paper or index card.

One passenger will mix up all the letters so they are not in order. They will pull a single letter and announce it to the car. Everyone, including the person who drew the letter, looks out the window to find something that begins with that letter. They call out what they see—for example, if the letter is B, people might spot bushes, a baseball field, Burger King, a BMW or branches.

After each passenger has said something that begins with the letter, move on and choose a new letter.

Make it easier

For kids who are still learning their ABCs, make the phonetic sound of the letter, too. You might also want to say an example of a word that starts with the letter.

If kids are still having trouble, help them by spotting something out the window and sounding out the word. They'll catch on and probably say the word before you get to the end.

Make it harder

Instead of moving on when everyone has spotted one thing that starts with the given letter, keep going. Each passenger takes a turn saying something that begins with the letter. The round ends when someone can't think of something or when someone says an item that has already been named before.

Then a new round, with a new letter, begins.

Fun Facts

History shows that in addition to inventing the lightning rod and bifocal glasses, the American inventor Benjamin Franklin wanted to edit the alphabet. He proposed simplifying it by removing C, J, Q, W and X, then adding 6 brand-new letters!

The letter E is the most common in the English language. It is used in more than 1 in 10 words.

6
Counting Cows

Categories:

- Numbers
- Competition
- Teamwork

Do you want your kids to be *really focused*—on something other than if they can watch another movie or if you are, indeed, there yet? Then Counting Cows is the attention magnet you need.

You can adapt this game to whatever farm animals are most common where you're driving. So if it works better, play Counting Sheep or Counting Llamas. (And if you're road tripping through a place where llamas are that common, tell me where!!!)

Directions

Imagine the car is divided in half lengthwise. The people on either side of the car become teams. The folks on the left side look out the left windows, and the passengers on the right side look out the right.

As you drive, keep an eye out for cows. Each cow is worth one point; keep track to tally how many points you have.

The twist: If you see a white horse, your score doubles. If you cross railroad tracks, everyone's score is reduced by half. The first team to spot a graveyard shouts "Ghost cow!" to make the other team lose all their points.

You can play until one team reaches a certain number of points you decide on beforehand. You can also play until everyone gets tired of cows.

Make it easier

Younger kids won't be able to count cows *and* keep track of points. So to play with littles, an adult keeps score while kids focus on the cows. If your kids get upset when their siblings win, you can play this game as a single team with no winners or losers.

Make it harder

Add a new rule every five minutes. (Set a timer to remind you.) Passengers take turns coming up with ways to increase or decrease points. Some ideas:

- Calves count for two points
- Farmers count for ten points
- When you go over a bridge, count out loud as fast as you can without skipping any numbers. When you reach the opposite end of the bridge, stop counting. The number you counted up to equals the number of bonus points you get.

Make these offbeat rules cumulative. So if you play the game multiple times, all the previous rules carry over.

Fun Facts

Scientists looking at satellite images discovered that cows have an "internal compass." They tend to align in a north-south direction, pointing their heads to either the north or south when they graze or sleep.

A cow's main stomach (of four digestive areas) can hold a bathtub's worth of food at a time.

Research shows that cows have best friends. A cow feels less stress and is actually smarter when it's with a buddy.

7
Y.E.S. N.O.

Categories:

- Competition
- Driver-safe

"No" is probably the last thing kids want to hear on a road trip. With this game, you won't actually say "no" to their questions, like Can we stop for ice cream? or Can we leave Sister at the next rest stop?

That's because in Y.E.S. N.O., no one in the car can say either "yes" or "no."

Are you wondering if this game is fun for the whole family? My answer is Y.E.S.

Directions

Begin the game by reminding everyone that they can't say "yes" or "no" but can use any synonym they like (yep, aye, nah, huh-uh).

Listen for when someone else says an off-limits word. If you're the first person to point it out, you get 10 points. If you accidentally said the word that shall not be named, you lose 5 points.

You can try to get each other to say "yes" or "no" by asking questions that don't seem related to the game.

Continue the game as long as you like. Or, if your road trip spans several days, don't ever stop! You'll forget at some point and get called out in the most unexpected moments, like when answering the drive-through person when they ask if you want ketchup with your fries.

Make it easier

Before you begin, brainstorm words you can say instead of "no" or "yes." I've found that little kids absolutely *crush* this game, so you probably won't have to adapt it for the young set.

Make it harder

Instead of playing by points, the person who caught someone saying a banned word gets to make up a new rule. They choose another word, gesture or noise that is forbidden during the game. For example, they might decide that no one can point (it's *really funny* to see what people come up with instead, like gesturing with their elbows or flourishing a hand).

Fun Facts

Many fields, from security to health care, use code words in place of other phrases. A captain will say "Pan-Pan" if their ship is in danger; someone in the military will say "WILCO" as a shortened version of "will comply;" and chefs will use the term "86" when a restaurant runs out of a menu item.

8
Graph Paper Battleship

Categories:

- Numbers
- Competition
- Printable

If you're like me, you probably remember the "*boop-boop-booboobooboo*" sound the classic game Battleship made as you tried to sink your opponent's boat. This version doesn't have the submarine sound effects, but it's still just as fun!

I also like this family road trip game because it's so portable. All you need is graph paper and a few pencils or pens. That means you can also play while the family is waiting in line at an amusement park, at the table after you've ordered your meal or as a quiet pre-bedtime game in a hotel room.

Directions

Use either the printables at ToAndFroFam.com/games or graph paper labeled with two identical grids (letters down the left side and numbers across the top). On one grid, each player marks down where their battleships are located. Depending on the size of your graph paper, you'll want to "hide" three or more boats of varying lengths on your board. The other grid represents your opponent's board.

Take turns guessing squares using the labeled grid (e.g. A-5 or C-8). The opponent says "hit" or "miss," depending on if a ship is located on that square. Keep track of the hits by coloring in that square; put an X through any squares where your opponent's boats aren't located.

Meanwhile, the person whose boat has been blasted marks the hit on their board. When all the squares on a boat have been hit, announce that the boat sunk.

Continue until one person's boats are all sunk.

Make it easier

My kids are not into battleships, and we don't actually let them play any games with guns. If that's the case in your family, adapt what's being hidden.

For example, my kids are currently obsessed with dragons and fairies. So they could "hide" dragons of different lengths in the "sky" (aka graph paper) or fairy homes in the forest. In this case, you'd probably want to customize what they say when one is found. You definitely don't want to hit and sink fairy houses!

Make it harder

Use graph paper with more squares and more ships to make this game even harder.

Fun Facts

The first submarine bought by the U.S. Navy cost $150,000. That's just a little more than what you'd pay for a personal jet pack these days.

Most ships have a unique motto, which crew would repeat to boost morale or inspire each other during a battle.

9
Mine/Yours/Ours

Categories:

- Driver-safe

Ready to leave your fate to chance? With this hilarious game, your life—where you live, what you'll eat for the rest of your life, even who your family is—is determined 100% by luck.

This activity gets the whole car laughing and is totally easy. There are no complicated rules to follow, no math to do, no spelling or ABCs—just good, old fashioned silliness.

Directions

Together, choose a category of things you'll see on the upcoming stretch of road trip. Some ideas:

- Billboards
- Houses
- Roadside attractions
- Animals
- Families in other cars
- Restaurants

One passenger begins. When they see the first example of the category, they say "mine;" the next is "yours," deciding who else in the car belongs to that example; the next one is "ours."

The next passenger playing takes over with another round of mine/yours/ours.

This can get silly—and random. For example, if you're using the billboards category, "mine" might be a swanky hotel, "yours" a can of dog food and "ours" a tulip farm.

There's no winning or losing in this game, but it can get everyone happily engaged in a shared activity.

Make it harder

Get more specific with the categories. Instead of looking for restaurants you pass to be a mine/yours/ours spot to lunch, add a twist. For example, the restaurant could serve the kind of food you'll have to eat for the rest of your life.

Fun Facts

In 76 countries worldwide, people drive on the left side of the road. That's about a third of the world's population.

10
Alphabetical Animals

Categories:

- Word games
- Memory
- Driver-safe

I'm guessing that your kids are like mine and grew up on alphabet animal books. You know the ones—A is for ape, B is for bear. My favorite alphabet animal book turned tradition on its head by naming totally random critters—G is for gnu, X is for xerus.

If you happened to read that one, too, pull out your extensive animal knowledge for this game! In it, you and your kids will practice letters and spelling as well as memory.

Directions

Everyone in the car will take turns matching a letter to an animal in alphabetical order, repeating all the animals that came before.

Someone might begin the game by saying, "A is for antelope." The next person would start by saying, "A is for antelope," then add an animal that begins with the following letter: "B is for badger." The third person repeats the animals for A and B, then adds C.

The game continues, adding on letters and animals as you go. By the end—Z—you'll have to say 26 animal names in alphabetical order!

Make it easier

Create a resource for your kids so they don't have to remember the order of all the letters. You can just write the alphabet on a piece of paper.

You can also play on teams, pairing an adult with younger kids. That way, a grown-up can gently nudge the child's memory or help them figure out what sound a P makes.

Make it harder

In addition to naming an animal, make its noise! You'll have to repeat each animal *and* its noise to keep the game going.

It'll sound like a noisy zoo in your car, and you'll crack up trying to make the sound of a giraffe or aardvark.

Fun Facts

X-ray fish isn't the only animal that starts with an X. There's the xerus (also called an African ground squirrel), Xantus's hummingbird, xenops (a brown insect-eating bird) and Xenarthra, which isn't technically an animal but is a group of critters that include sloths, armadillos and anteaters.

Some animals have wacky names. Consider the screaming hairy armadillo, wunderpus (a type of octopus) and tasseled wobbegong (a shark that lives in the waters near Australia and New Guinea).

11
Vanity Plates

Categories:

- Word games
- Driver-safe
- Out the window

On your road trip, you'll definitely come across a few vanity plates—you know, when folks pay extra to have something special spelled on their car's license plate. This game pretends that *every* vehicle on the road shares a message via its plates.

Directions

Passengers take turns transforming the random combination of letters on a nearby car's license plate into an abbreviated message, name or phrase.

One way to do this: Imagine that the license plate is an acronym (aka a shortened way of saying something by using the first letter of each word in a phrase). That is, each letter in the license plate stands for a word. So if you saw the license EDS, you might say it stands for "Elephants Drive Sportscars."

You can also imagine the license as a shortened way of spelling a word, like BPKN = Bumpkin. It's funny to think of how these words or phrases relate to the driver and invent why they chose that as their vanity plate.

Make it easier

Instead of trying to make a phrase, just pick words that begin with each letter in the license plate. They won't necessarily form anything coherent, but it's a great way for younger kids to participate and practice their letters.

Make it harder

To play a competitive version, one person picks a license plate on a nearby car. Everyone else playing the game makes up a phrase or word that the plates stand for. After all passengers have shared their made-up message, the first person picks their favorite and awards a point to the winner. The person who ends up with the most points wins.

Fun Facts

The earliest license plates were made out of porcelain, the material of some vases. Imagine how fragile they must have been!

The letters I, O and Q are seldom used on a license plate, probably because they look too much like numbers.

12
Tally the Trucks

Categories:

- Numbers
- Printable

Most people know the game Slug Bug (called many other names): Whenever you pass a VW bug, you punch your seatmate in the arm. When I was growing up in a college town much beloved by hippies, we had plenty of VW Vanagons driving around, too. So we doubled the punching opportunities by yelling "Box sox!" whenever we saw one.

Tally the Trucks is an activity that carries on that car-spotting tradition but with a lot fewer bruises.

Directions

Print your free copy of the Tally the Trucks printable at ToAndFroFam.com/games, or create your own version using graph paper. Kids will then color in a square for each item they find in a handful of categories.

On my printable, you'll see categories like yellow car and blue truck. You'll also notice that a few sections are blank so you can add categories that will most interest your kids.

What's more, I created an entirely blank template (also downloadable) so you can customize it for your kids. That way, if they're not interested in cars at all but love animals, you could make a section for hawks, crows, cows, horses and so forth.

This activity keeps kids occupied for as long as they still have squares to fill. Plus, it's a totally fun way for young kids to practice math skills.

Make it easier

Work on one category at a time. So try to fill in all the squares in the first category first, then move on to the next category.

Make it harder

Customize the printable with more complex clues, like "road sign that includes a Z" or "coffee joint that isn't Starbucks."

Fun Facts

An estimated 15.5 million big trucks drive around the U.S., delivering everything from potatoes and lumber to t-shirts and even other trucks!

Roughly 60% of cars in the U.S. are either black, white or gray. Yellow is the least popular color.

13
MASH For Kids

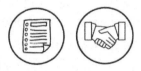

Categories:

- Printable
- Teamwork

When I was growing up, MASH was the most popular game on the elementary school playground. With a few minor adaptations, it'll be a hit with your kids, too.

I made this version less focused on romance (I mean, why do we want children predicting who they'll marry?!). And hey, if you and any other adults on the road trip get bored, play your own version. Who knows, the game might foretell that you're destined to move into a mansion!

Directions

Print out the MASH For Kids printable at ToAndFroFam.com/games or draw your own. Choose one person to have their fortune told. The fortune teller fills out the MASH sheet.

For each category, the first person fills in half of the blanks, and the fortune teller picks the other half. The fortune teller can make their choices as silly as they want!

When all the blanks are filled out, the fortune teller begins to draw a spiral (starting from the inside and expanding outward). The person having their fortune told says "stop" whenever they want, at which point the fortune teller stops drawing. The fortune teller then comes to the "magic number" by counting across the spiral, starting at the end and crossing to the other side. The "magic number" comes from how many lines they cross.

Beginning with the M in MASH, the fortune teller counts as they point from option to option in a clockwise direction. When they reach the "magic number," they cross off that entry. Continue clockwise around the MASH sheet, skipping the crossed-out options.

Once a category has only one option left, circle it. Continue until all categories have one option circled.

The activity ends with the fortune teller looking into the other person's future. They can tell a story of what will happen, using the circled options to foretell their destiny.

Note: You may want to remind your kids that this is only a game and doesn't actually mean anything in real life.

Also, MASH traditionally stands for Mansion, Apartment, Shack, House. If your kids would be upset about living in a shack, you can change the S to Swimming Pool for a sillier option.

Make it easier

If the spiral drawing feels too complicated, just ask the other person for their favorite number. Use that as the "magic number."

An adult can also help fill in the categories, leaving the kids to count and tell the fortune at the end.

Make it harder

For a longer game, add more categories. Kids can come up with their own based on their interests. Ideas for extra categories:

- Go-to vacation spot
- Type of transportation used to get to work
- Major in college
- Biggest accomplishment

Fun Facts

People have tried to peek into the future for centuries, using all sorts of methods. Fortune tellers read tea leaves, looked to the stars, swung a necklace or other pendulum, examined the lines on someone's palm and gazed into a crystal ball.

The origami fortune teller is a fun way for kids to answer questions, share funny messages or, yes, glimpse into the future. This folded paper is called by many names, including chatterbox, cootie catcher and flip-flapper.

14
I Spy

Categories:

- Driver-safe
- Out the window

Directions

The first person to go, aka the "spy-er," spots something inside or outside the car. They then give one clue about the item. They share this clue by saying, "I spy with my little eye something that is…" This can be the color of the item (the standard clue) or any other characteristic, such as what material it's made of or what letter it starts with.

The other players try to guess what the item is. You don't need to go in a certain order or take turns; simply call out ideas, popcorn-style.

The person who guesses the item correctly is the next "spy-er."

Make it easier

Establish a few limits, like the item must be inside the car. This narrows down the options.

You can also give multiple clues. Try, "I spy with my little eye something that is white, fluffy and shaped like an alligator!"

Additionally, if younger kids get frustrated that they can't correctly guess the item, throw them a softball: Pick something they're likely to see and think of almost immediately.

Make it harder

Pretend your eyes are a camera taking a mental snapshot of the scenery. The spy-er gives the players a warning when they're about to take this snapshot. The spy-er picks something from that particular sliver of scenery, aka the snapshot. Just as in the regular version, the spy-er gives a clue about what they're thinking of.

The other players then have to visualize the snapshot of scenery, searching their memory for things that match that clue, since it may not be visible anymore. This is much harder and is also great practice for observation and memory!

Fun Facts

Speaking of real spies, the intelligence-gathering agency in the United States used cameras attached to pigeons to get information from places where people couldn't safely go.

15
Trip-Themed
Word Search

Categories:

- Word games

Your kids are probably not into searching for a parking spot or an upcoming rest area, but I'm pretty sure they *will* love word searches. Now the internet makes it super-simple to create your own personalized versions of this classic kids' activity.

Simply type in a few words or phrases related to your destination or trip. Your kids will be mega impressed. Don't worry, I won't tell them creating a custom word search just took a few clicks.

Directions

Go to a word search generator online, such as WorksheetWorks.com. Enter words related to your route, destination or even family inside jokes. I recommend using a minimum of 10 words or short phrases.

Click the "create" or "generate" button on the word search generator, then download the PDF. Print copies before you leave home.

You can also create different word searches for the stages of your trip. You might make a word search for every state you'll pass through, the major destinations or car-related phrases.

Make it easier

Use fewer words, use the option for capital letters and make sure to click the option of orienting words vertically and horizontally but not diagonally.

Make it harder

Increase the number of words as well as letters across (a 20x20 letter word search starts to get challenging!). Include options to orient words diagonally *and* backwards. If your kids are learning a language, try a word search in that tongue!

Fun Facts

Do you know what "dord" means? No? Well, neither does anyone else. This "ghost word" appeared in an English dictionary in the 1930s because of a typo. It doesn't have a definition.

An "ambigram" is a word that can be read upside down, like SWIMS.

16
Nickel Scenery

Categories:

- Competition
- Printable

Penny for your thoughts… and nickel for your eagle eyes! In this high stakes but low cost road trip game, the first person to spot an item on the list wins… a whole 5 cents.

Before you roll your eyes, think back to when you were a kid. Remember when you'd scrounge in the couch cushions and the cup holders in your parents' car for a few coins? Your kids will relive that excitement and get a zing of reward for every nickel they win.

Another reason I love this game: You don't have to prep, and you can introduce it any time your kids are getting antsy. Even if you don't come up with a list ahead of time, you can just call out the next item to find.

Just don't use up all your toll money!

Directions

Make a list of items you're likely to spot on your road trip, or use the printable available at ToAndFroFam.com/games. These should be easily seen from your kids' vantage point in the back seat.

As you drive, call out the first item on your list—hay bale, mile marker, car with a stuffed animal in its back window, whatever! Your kids will need to look out the window to find the item. The first person to see it gets a nickel.

Continue as long as you like (or as long as you still have change!).

Note: This is a lot harder for kids in the middle seat, since they can't see out the window as well.

Make it easier

Instead of reading from a list of items to spot out the window, look down the road for an item that's coming up in a few seconds. Your kids will love the immediacy of finding it right away!

If your kids want *everything* to be equal, pick items on alternating sides of the road. That way, they'll end up with the same number of nickels.

Make it harder

Instead of naming the item the kids are hunting for, give them a clue. So "hay bale" could be "something that makes Mom sneeze" or "a big hunk of horse food."

Fun Facts

The American nickel replaced two other five-cent pieces: the half-dime, which people often lost because of its tiny size, and the five-cent bill. Can you imagine shelling out 20 five-cent bills to make a dollar?

It costs nearly 8 cents for the U.S. Mint to make a nickel.

17
Thought Bubbles

Categories:

- Driver-safe
- Out the window

Ever wish you could read minds? In this game, you'll pretend you can.

As you pass people on the highway, your crew will test their imagination. Who can come up with the wackiest, most laughable or most likely thought bubble?

Directions

Pick a passenger to start the game. Someone else looks out the window and chooses a person, family or even animal. The other person uses their turn by imagining what the person (or critter!) in the car or on the road is thinking. This is the "thought bubble," just like the ones in a comic book.

This can be especially fun when other cars on the road are full. It can be hilarious to come up with thought bubbles for each person, creating a whole scenario inside the vehicle.

I particularly like this game for when traffic is slow. You'll have the opportunity to take a good look at the other people on the road before you invent their thought bubbles. Just don't get caught staring!

Make it easier

Play this game collaboratively. Littles and shy kids may have an easier time coming up with someone else's thoughts when they do it together with their family.

Make it harder

To up the ante, decide on an award for each passenger's turn. You might deem someone's thought bubble Most Likely To Cause A Family Argument, Nicest Imaginary Conversation or Most Likely to

Actually Be Aliens in the Car. Let your creativity shine!

Fun Facts

Does your road trip feel never-ending? Just imagine if you tried to drive to the sun! It would take you 150 years to arrive.

Roughly 4 in 10 drivers name their car.

18
Law & Disorder

Categories:

- Driver-safe
- Printable

You know the basic rules of the road: Stop at red lights, yield to pedestrians, obey the speed limit (ish). Chances are you *don't* know about the many strange traffic laws within the United States.

Take, for example, these head scratchers:

- It's illegal to ride a camel on the highway in Arizona
- In Missouri, you can't drive with an uncaged bear in your car
- No fuzzy dice hanging from the rearview mirror in Illinois; it's illegal there

Can you come up with stranger laws? Play this game to find out.

Directions

Before you leave, print and cut out the Law & Disorder printable found at ToAndFroFam.com/ games. Mix them up as if they were a deck of cards, or put them all into a baggie or hat.

The first person to play selects two cards. Each card will have a picture of a random object or action on it. These cards are not labeled, so they're open to interpretation.

That person must invent a law that somehow relates to *both* the cards they've chosen. Play then moves to the next passenger (well, as soon as everyone stops laughing).

Clearly, the driver can't draw and look at cards. Someone else in the car can pick for the driver and explain what the pictures show.

Make it easier

You can make up a law that relates to just one of the cards you pull.

You can also try these formulas:

It is illegal to _____ during _____.
It is illegal to _____ at _____.
It is illegal to use _____ while _____.
You must _____ when _____.

Make it harder

Want a little competition? Try this variation.

One person draws two cards and announces them to the car. Every other passenger invents a law that includes both of the cards. The person who picked the cards chooses their favorite law. Play then moves to the next person.

Fun Facts

People in Mississippi aren't allowed to drive with a flamethrower attached to the car. Does that make it legal in all other 49 states?

In Cyprus, it's illegal to eat or drink while driving.

19
Start to End Geography

Categories:

- Driver-safe
- Word games

This place names game is a fun mental workout, even if you've never won a spelling bee or if geography wasn't your best subject. I particularly like this game for when the scenery is d-u-l-l, since it doesn't require an interesting landscape or even road signs.

Ready to rev up those brain cells? Let's go.

Directions

One person begins the game by naming a place. This can be a country, state, city, river or other geographic feature. The last letter of that place must be the first letter of the next person's named place.

So if the first person named Kentucky, the final letter is Y—so the next person has to think up a place that begins with Y, such as Yemen. The next person has to think of a place that starts with N, and so forth.

Make it easier

Young kids who struggle to think up place names can say any word that begins with the final letter of the previous place name. Everyone else who is able has to stick with place names.

Make it harder

Geography whizzes can add a challenge by sticking within a category, such as bodies of water, places in South America or capital cities.

Just be ready to fact check wily passengers. My dad once came up with the Welsh Sea, which he *still* claims is a real place decades after the fact, in spite of it 100% not existing.

Fun Facts

The longest place name in the world takes 85 letters to spell. Taumatawhakatangihangakoauauotamateaturi pukakapikimaungahoronukupokaiwhenuakitanatahu is a small hill on the northern island of New Zealand. Even the locals call it by a nickname, Taumata, which only contains 7 letters.

You might wonder what got into the folks who named these odd places: Eggs and Bacon Bay, Tasmania; Punkeydoodles Corners, Ontario, Canada; and Boring, Oregon, U.S.

20
Road Sign
Alphabet Game

Categories:

- Word games
- Out the window

To summarize the Cheshire Cat in Lewis Carroll's *Alice in Wonderland,* if you don't know where you want to end up, it doesn't much matter which direction you go. While I admire the cat's carefree wanderlust, *you* have a destination in mind.

And it's *not* the many, many, many places you pass along the way.

That said, all those not-destinations do have a purpose: Their signage is great for this classic road trip game. In the Road Sign Alphabet Game, players pay close attention to what would otherwise be never-noticed places.

Directions

Starting with A, players look for road signs that contain each letter in the alphabet, in order. You cannot count a sign that contains a letter until the previous letter has been found. That's to say, if you haven't found a sign with G in it, you can't count a sign for H.

The first person to Z wins.

Make it easier

In this variation, the family works together. (Many eyes are better than two!) You may want to write out the alphabet for kids still learning their ABCs. They'll use the resource to figure out what letter comes next.

Make it harder

Instead of looking for a letter anywhere in the sign, a word must *begin* with the letter in order to count. So for A, "bank" couldn't count, but "Applebee's" would.

Fun Facts

The American William Phelps Eno is credited with coming up with the concept of a stop sign, yet he never drove in his life—not even once.

Interstate highway signs in the U.S. are green because more than half of people surveyed preferred the color over blue or black.

21
Next Song

Categories:

- Driver-safe
- Music

Have you ever taken a road trip with the annoying kind of passenger who constantly flips through radio stations or playlists? One word: unacceptable.

But in this game, switching songs before the last note *is* allowed. Before you fast forward through this game, take a look at the instructions below. You may just want to include this activity in your playlist.

Directions

The designated DJ cues up a playlist, either on their phone or a mix CD. Before you hit "play," everyone in the car chooses a word. It can be anything, from super-common words (like "the" or "it") to more random ones (e.g. "heart," "bounce" or "air").

As soon as everyone picks and announces their word, choose the random option on your music app, playlist or CD player, then push play.

Everyone listens carefully to the lyrics. The first person to hear their chosen word shouts it out, then "Next song!"

The DJ presses pause. Everyone chooses a new word. The catch—you can't pick a word that someone else used before. Then the DJ pushes skip to move on to the next song.

Make it easier

Instead of using a random mix of songs, use a CD or album your whole family listens to all the time. (We've listened to the *Frozen* soundtrack so many times I often wake up with those songs stuck in my head.)

Push the random play option so no one knows what track is coming next. Narrowing down the potential songs makes it easier to think up a word that's likely to be in the next tune.

Make it harder

Instead of using your own music, turn to the radio. And instead of skipping to the next song, use your car radio's search function to move to the next station. Listen for the word you chose, even if you ended up tuning into a hosted talk show or news program.

You never know what genre you'll flip to next, so playing by random radio stations makes this game more challenging!

Fun Facts

When you don't count common words like "I," "you" and "the," "love" shows up most frequently in all musical genres except rap and heavy metal. In rap, "got" is most popular, and in heavy metal, "life" tops the charts.

In the USSR, a popular *The Voice*-type singing show relied on watchers to weigh in on their favorite performers—by turning their lights on or off. Since most families didn't own a phone, they'd flip the lights on if they liked a song and went dark when they didn't. The local power company measured the energy usage to determine the most popular tune (and the show's winner).

22
Meet in the Middle

Categories:

- Word games
- Driver-safe

Do great minds think alike? At the very least, do family minds think alike? Try this game and you might find your answer.

On the surface, it might seem like it would take *forever* to successfully complete a round of Meet in the Middle. You might be surprised at how quickly some rounds go! Give it a try and see how totally random thoughts can, in fact, meet on common ground.

Directions

In this two-player game, each person says a random word on the count of three. The players then take a moment to think up what the two words have in common. On the count of three, the players say this word in common out loud. For example, if the players said "flamingo" and "bathtub," one person might say "water" and the other could say "foot" (since flamingos often stand on one foot and a fancy bath is a claw foot tub).

Don't be surprised if you have to explain your train of thought!

Next, they pause to think up what the next set of words has in common. Continuing the previous example, on the count of three they might say "sandal" and "footprint." That might lead both people to come up with "beach."

Make it easier

Start with a common category, such as food or school. That way, the random words you pick won't be entirely unrelated.

Make it harder

Think fast! Put a time limit on how long you have to think up your connecting word. Whoever fails to think up a word in time gets a strike. After a player gets three strikes, someone else gets to challenge the winner.

Fun Facts

You don't have to be artistic to be creative. As Apple founder Steve Jobs said, "Creativity is just connecting things." Seeing links between seemingly unrelated words is an excellent way to exercise your creativity muscle.

How's this for seemingly unconnected things: Research shows that people who can wait longer to use the bathroom also tend to be better at saving money. So does that make camels the biggest penny pinchers?

23
20 Questions

Categories:

- Driver-safe
- Guessing

There's a reason this road trip game has been around since cavekids were asking their caveparents, "Are we there yet?" It's a classic in part because of its ease and adaptability. Kids can choose whatever they're interested in, from superheroes to supernovas, and the game can be played anywhere.

See if this game will stand the test of time with your own family.

Directions

The first person chooses a mystery item the rest of the passengers will try to identify. Once they've chosen, they announce what category it fits into—person, place or thing.

The other passengers take turns asking yes or no questions to narrow down what the mystery item could be. If the category were *person*, they might ask, "Is this person a celebrity? Is this person a man? Is this person someone we know personally?"

The passenger who has chosen the mystery object keeps track of the number of questions asked. This is easy to do by counting on your fingers. Once you've gone through all 10 fingers twice, the game is over.

If the guessers figure out the mystery object before their allotted questions run out, they win. If not, the person who chose the mystery object wins.

Make it easier

The person who chooses the mystery object gives a clue when the guessers have asked 5, 10 and then 15 questions.

Make it harder

Play a speed round! Ask and answer the questions as quickly as you possibly can.

Fun Facts

Statistically, four-year-old girls ask the most questions of anyone: They average 390 per day, which is about one question every two minutes while they're awake!

When you learn new information as a result of asking a question, you're more likely to remember it. So you actually build up your knowledge more quickly by asking those Qs!

24
Alternate Titles

Categories:

- Driver-safe
- Word games
- Guessing

You know that family blockbuster *Unshaven Urn-Maker and the Chalice of Flame*? No? How about *Harry Potter and the Goblet of Fire*?

In this game, your family will take turns making up alternate titles to books or movies you know and love.

What's more, this road trip game is a fun way to expand vocabulary and teach younger kids about synonyms. Plus, they're practically guaranteed to make you giggle.

Directions

One person begins by choosing a movie or book title the other people in the car are likely to know. They then think up synonyms to replace the words in the title, trying to match the number of words to the original. So *Frozen* could be *Chilled* and *Cat in the Hat* could be *Feline in a Fedora*.

The other passengers try to figure out the original title. The first person who guesses it correctly comes up with the next alternate title.

Make it easier

Narrow down the categories. For example, you could take turns creating alternate titles for Disney flicks or Marvel Universe movies.

Make it harder

Commit to playing three rounds of the game. Each player thinks up a theme that connects the three titles. The other passengers have to guess the connecting theme.

Fun Facts

The wildly popular movie *E.T.* was originally titled *Night Skies*, then *A Boy's Life*, before landing on its now-famous name.

"Euphemism" is a synonym, or word, that is a more polite word for standing in for something inappropriate or harsh. Can you think of a few examples?

25
Word by Word

Categories:

- Driver-safe
- Music

So you've listened to the *Moana* soundtrack so many times you can sing each song in your sleep. But what if you had to ID the movie's most popular song by just the first word, "I've"? How about the first two, "I've been"? Would it take you three words—"I've been staring"?

Test you and your kids' music memorization with this fun game.

Directions

The first person decides on a song everyone will know. They begin by saying the first word of the song's lyrics. They continue adding a word, one by one, until the other passengers correctly guess it or give up.

The game continues either in clockwise direction, or the turn moves to the person who correctly identified the song.

Make it easier

Instead of simply saying each word, sing each word with the tune. The songs will be easier to recognize when they're set to the original melody.

Make it harder

Decide on a number of rounds or songs to play in the game. Keep score of who correctly guesses the most songs. The winner gets to play DJ in the car!

Fun Facts

The oldest piece of music ever discovered was written down in 1500 BC. It was found in Mesopotamia, in what is now Iraq.

When people sing together, their hearts are more likely to beat in time. Research shows that choir singers' heart rates become similar—speeding up or slowing down at the same time.

26
Sweet or Sour

Categories:

- Guessing
- Teamwork
- Out the window

One of the best parts of travel is meeting new people—something you can even do while driving. Sort of.

Here, you'll turn this into a game by waving at folks you pass on the road. Will they wave back?

One reason I like this game is it takes the focus off the *inside* of the car, which is excellent if kids are getting on each other's nerves. There are also endless variations, some of which I'll cover below, that involve math and estimating!

Will you make friends on your next road trip? Play this game and find out.

Directions

Together, pick a car, pedestrian or other person you see outside. As a group, wave to them. (The driver shouldn't do this if it's unsafe.)

If they wave back, they count as "sweet." If they don't wave back, they count as "sour."

Keep track of how many sweets you get vs. sours. Will friendly folks win the day? Or will the grouches outnumber them?

Make it easier

This game is already super easy: Even toddlers can play! You can mix things up by taking turns choosing different "greetings." Instead of a wave, you might flap your arms like a chicken, have an in-seat dance party or make your hands into binoculars to peer at the passing cars. Will other people gesture back at you?

Make it harder

Decide on a time limit for the game—5 or 10 minutes, for example. Each passenger predicts if they'll see more sweets or sours. Tally the sweets and sours to see how many of each you have by the end of the time period. The people who estimated correctly win.

Alternatively, you can bet on each group you wave to. Start by picking a carful of people or a pedestrian. Each player bets if the group will be sweet or sour. If you bet correctly, you get a point. If you bet incorrectly, you lose a point. The person with the most points at the end wins.

Fun Facts

A wave can have different meanings in different cultures. In Japan, waving near your face can mean that you don't understand; in Deaf communities, waving while wiggling your fingers can mean applause.

27
Poetry in Motion

  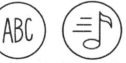

Categories:

- Driver-safe
- Word games
- Music
- Teamwork

Could it be that you're a poet and you don't even know it? Or that you can sing in the car as you drive from near to far?

In this road trip game, you'll attempt to do both.

This collaborative game will have you writing a poem, song or rap—together.

Directions

One person begins by starting with a phrase. It can be anything; it's often fun to begin a story or say something that relates to what you're doing. The next person says another phrase that continues the idea of the first. The trick: The final word of that phrase must rhyme with the previous phrase.

The next person says another phrase, which doesn't have to rhyme with the previous one. The fourth person completes that idea with a rhyming phrase. They should all relate to each other, just as a song, poem or rap sticks to a common theme or narrative.

For example, a round might begin like this:

We were driving down the road, yeah we were driving down the highway /
We passed a hitchhiker. He asked, "Are you going my way?"

The hitchhiker hopped in and buckled up his seat belt /
But then his face turned pale and green. I asked him how he felt.

Continue as long as you like, or until you feel like your poem/song is complete.

*Note: This game works best with an odd number of players. That way, everyone gets a turn starting and completing the rhymes.

Make it easier

The shorter the phrase, the easier it is to rhyme. You might try something like:

> I see a lot of trees /
> I want to climb one, please.

> I hear some cows go *moo* /
> Are we driving to the zoo?

Don't worry too much about the lyrics making sense or adding up to a coherent poem. With younger kids, it's just fun to rhyme!

Make it harder

One passenger can look up and play instrumental beats on their phone. This music will be the backbone of your song or rap.

The challenge: Come up with lyrics that fit the beat *and* say them before the next verse starts!

Fun Facts

Humans have used rhyme in music and spoken word for millennia. It both sounds nice to the ear and helps with memorization.

A handful of words in English don't have a perfect rhyme, but you can still match them to similar sounding words. For example, you could pair *orange* and *door hinge* or *purple* and *whirlpool*. This is called a "slant rhyme."

28
Group Effort Storytelling

Categories:

- Driver-safe
- Teamwork
- Word games
- Printable

You know when your kid says, does or asks something totally out of the blue? Like when you're making dinner and your little asks where the end of the universe is? Or when you're driving along and they suddenly announce what they want to be for Halloween?

Those non-sequiturs—aka something unrelated to the previous thing—are just part of the game here!

You'll use the printable from a previous road trip game, Law & Disorder (game #18), that will take your stories to unexpected places. You can download this printable for free at ToAndFroFam.com/games.

Directions

Before you leave home, print and cut out the Law & Disorder printable; keep the squares in a baggie. To begin, one person starts a story. It can begin "Once upon a time…" or "The other day I…" or however else you'd like. That person continues for a few sentences.

When they're done with their part of the story, they include a transition for the next person. Here are some ideas for transitions:

- Then…
- To her surprise…
- All of a sudden…
- Next…
- In the meantime…
- After that…
- Soon…
- Later that day…
- Before he knew it…
- The following day…

The next person pulls a square from the baggie. They continue the story—and have to incorporate whatever the square represents into the next part.

For example, if the first person began, "Once upon a time, there was a tiger who thought she was a llama. So she began eating grass. Little did she know, …"

If the next person pulled a square with a bicycle on it, they might continue, "Little did she know, she was actually a new species of bicycle-riding llama that just looked like a tiger! She rode her bike to the nearby llama farm."

And so on. You may want to write down these hilarious stories because you'll never want to forget them!

Make it easier

Kids tend to take to this game really easily. They're natural storytellers and already have inventive imaginations!

If kids (or adults!) are having trouble, come up with the next part of the story as a team.

Make it harder

Instead of picking one square, pick two. You have to incorporate *both* items into your part of the story.

Fun Facts

The United Nations cultural agency UNESCO estimates that more than 2 million new books are published every year. The country that publishes the most? China. Will your story ever make it to print?

When you listen to a good story, your body releases the feel-good chemical oxytocin. Nicknamed the love hormone, oxytocin is involved in empathy, bonding with others and building relationships.

29
Doodle Telephone

Categories:

- Teamwork
- Printable

Remember the game Telephone? You might have played it at sleepovers or on the school bus. Basically, you whispered a random or funny phrase to the person next to you, who whispered to the next person what they *think* you said, and so on—often resulting in a garbled message by the end.

Although your kids may not relate to the crummy connection of a land line, I'm pretty sure they *will* connect to this silly adaptation of Telephone.

Note: This is definitely not a driver-safe game. People who get car sick should not play. On the other hand, Doodle Telephone is a terrific game to play when you want a little bit of quiet. Finally, this is one of my family's all-time favorite games. We particularly love to play it when we're at a restaurant waiting for food!

Directions

You'll need at least three people (not counting the driver) to play this game.

Before you leave home, print enough copies of the Doodle Telephone printable (at ToAndFroFam.com/games) for each passenger to have their own. You can also use a blank sheet of paper.

The game begins by everyone writing a phrase or sentence at the top of the Doodle Telephone page, in spot 1. Everyone passes their sheet in a clockwise direction to the next person. Everyone then draws the phrase or sentence from spot 1 in the next available space, spot 2. They then fold along the dotted line between spot 1 and spot 2 so spot 1 is hidden.

Pass the sheet clockwise. Everyone then looks at the drawing and writes what they think is happening, in spot 3. If you have more passengers who are playing, fold on the dotted line between spot 2 and spot 3 so the drawing in spot 2 is hidden.

Pass the sheet clockwise again. In spot 4, everyone draws the phrase or sentence written in spot 3.

Continue alternating between writing and drawing, folding over the previous spot so it's not visible, for as many turns as there are players.

When the sheet returns to its original owner, everyone opens up the folds to see how the phrase changed from the beginning to the end. Did anything get lost in translation?

Note: It's ok if your drawings aren't good enough to hang in a museum, or if they turn out wobbly from when the car hits a pot hole. That just adds to the fun!

Make it easier

Instead of writing a phrase or sentence, write a single word.

Make it harder

Play a game of Speed Doodle Telephone! Set a recurring timer for 30 or even 20 seconds. You won't have long to draw or figure out what the previous doodle represents!

Fun Facts

The cereal company Kellogg once tried to sell one of its products, Bran Buds, in Sweden. They then found out the name translated roughly to "burned farmer" and had to be changed!

30
Categories

Categories:

- Driver-safe
- Memory
- Competition

I'm betting your kids are geniuses about at least one topic. Maybe they can name approximately eleventy billion different dinosaurs or every Jojo Siwa song ever recorded. You're probably an expert on a handful of topics, too, from James Bond movies to sushi rolls.

The game of Categories will test everyone's knowledge of different groups of items. Just watch out: Kids often turn out to be little walking encyclopedias!

Directions

One person starts the game by choosing a category. This can be anything that has many items within it. A few examples of categories:

- Breeds of dogs
- Ice cream flavors
- Things that are hot
- Fruits
- States
- Professional baseball teams
- Things that start with D

Going in a clockwise direction, each person says one item within the chosen category. For example, if you're playing the category countries, people might name Iceland, Nigeria and Malaysia.

The key is to remember what everyone before you named because if you repeat an item, you're out!

Continue taking turns naming items within the category until someone is stumped. The remaining person is the winner.

Make it easier

Make sure to pick categories your kids will know. My younger daughter Maxine doesn't quite know which animals are mammals, for example, so I wouldn't choose mammals as a category.

Make it harder

Want to engage your whole brain? Play Categories while keeping a rhythm.

Everyone (except for the driver) makes a pattern of sound like this: lap slap, lap slap, clap, snap. This makes a four-count rhythm. Repeat this pattern continually, creating a steady beat.

The challenge is to say your item within the category *on the snap*. So you not only have to think up something within the category that hasn't been said before; you also have to say it at the right time. If you miss the beat, you're out!

Fun Facts

Insects are the most diverse group of animals. There are more than a million named insects that have been discovered so far, and researchers estimate that's just a fraction of the creepy crawlies out there!

The nonprofit The Nature Conservancy has trained an artificial intelligence tool to categorize social media photos that are taken underwater. They then use the number of snorkeling and scuba diving pictures to calculate how much money these underwater activities bring to local businesses. The nonprofit uses this categorization to persuade towns to protect ocean habitats!

31
Plot Twist

Categories:

- Teamwork
- Driver-safe
- Word games

You know that whiplash feeling when a movie or book throws a complete plot twist into the narrative? Brace yourself, because this game is going take you through more twists and turns than a M. Night Shyamalan movie.

Directions

One person begins by starting a story. They say a few sentences then yell, "Plot twist!" That's the cue for the next person to take the story in a totally different, totally unexpected direction. After a few sentences, this person then yells, "Plot twist!" Person 3 continues the story.

The game might go something like this: Player 1 begins, "A boy named Bill was walking to school one day. He reached into his backpack and then—plot twist!" The next person would think up something unexpected, like "And then Bill realized that the sandwich his mom packed for his lunch had come to life!"

Turns continue until one player says "The end."

Make it easier

Limit each person's contribution to one sentence. This will keep the game moving quickly, helping keep the attention of younger kids.

Make it harder

You can place limitations on what can happen, like making the story realistic fiction. That means that everything that happens in the story could actually happen in real life. (Alas, no sandwiches that come alive!)

Alternatively, you can keep a single game of Plot Twist going for ages. Simply pause anytime players start to get bored. You'll end on a cliffhanger (like "Then—plot twist!—the swamp monster came back to life!"), which will make restarting the game that much more fun.

The challenge in this version is to keep the game going as long as you can.

Fun Facts

A shaggy dog story is a long-winded tale that keeps people listening attentively—and has a disappointing, uneventful ending. Folks tell shaggy dog stories as a joke!

The phrase "That's All Folks" signaled the end of an episode of Looney Tunes, a cartoon popular in the 1930s and 1940s. The character Porky Pig repeated this phrase more than 100 times over the course of his "career" in cartoons.

32
Teamwork Art

Categories:

- Teamwork

As the iconic painter Pablo Picasso said, "Every child is an artist. The problem is how to remain an artist once he grows up."

This game is the solution to that problem! (Well, at least for the length of the game.)

No matter if you consider yourself a decent artist or not, you'll enjoy this collaborative drawing game.

Directions

Every player starts with a blank sheet of paper. (It's best to rest the paper on a book, clipboard or other hard surface.)

The driver, who of course can't safely draw, says a random noun (remember—a person, place or thing). Each player draws that on their paper.

Once everyone is finished drawing, pass the sheet of paper to the person to your left. The driver then says another random noun. Each player adds a drawing of that person, place or thing to their paper, incorporating it into the piece of "art."

Continue passing and drawing until one person is completely out of room on their paper. Then take a moment to admire your collaborative masterpieces!

Make it easier

The driver can pick things that younger artists are most comfortable drawing. If your little is an expert at sketching cats or cars, then use that as one of your nouns.

Make it harder

You can of course make this game more challenging by picking hard-to-draw items. (How does one draw a platypus?!) Each person's attempts will turn out to be hilarious!

Fun Facts

The art form Tunisian Collaborative Painting began in Tunisia as a way to preserve artists' free expression. In this method, a group of artists paints on a single canvas simultaneously without making a plan beforehand. They never know what the final piece will look like!

Leonardo da Vinci worked on Mona Lisa's smile for 16 years.

33
Department of Silly Rules

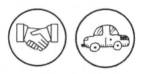

Categories:

- Teamwork
- Driver-safe

I'm not going to gloss over it: This game is straight-up ridiculous. (Yep, I saved the wackiest game for last.)

The Department of Silly Rules builds on itself, getting sillier and sillier as your road trip goes on. It also is one that you'll totally forget about until someone breaks a rule—or invents a new one!

But know this: Once you play this game, road trips will never be the same!

Directions

Before the game begins, decide the order in which passengers will make up rules. (You can go from youngest to oldest, for example, or play rock-paper-scissors to establish who's first.)

Next, tell your phone to set a timer to go off randomly. It will probably ask you for how long. Set the extended time for as long as you're traveling that day.

After a little while, the alarm will sound. This is the cue for the first player to create a silly rule.

This can be just about *anything* (as long as it's safe and within family rules, of course). Some examples:

- Hop 3 times whenever you get out of the car
- You can't say the word "you"
- Cluck like a chicken whenever you pass a farm
- Pretend to be super-fancy royalty whenever you eat or drink something

Whenever someone is caught slipping up, the person to call them out gets a point or little prize. (It's fun to give out a quarter to the person who catches the mistake, which they can save up and spend on a souvenir.)

You never know when the timer will signal the creation of a new rule, and you never know what your kids will come up with!

Make it easier

For people who don't like the winning/losing dynamic, don't keep score or award prizes to people who catch mistakes.

You can also play this game for a shorter period of time, like over the course of an hour.

Make it harder

Play this game throughout your entire road trip. You'll soon forget you're playing—that is, until someone notices you're breaking one of the silly rules!

Fun Facts

One silly rule in baseball: If a pitch gets stuck in the catcher's mask, all the players on base move forward one base.

Another strange one: It's against the rules to catch a ball in your hat. If you do, the batter automatically advances to third base.

Conclusion

I couldn't even begin to tally up how many miles my family and I have traveled together. At this point, both my kids *and* my dogs clamor to get into our minivan as soon as they possibly can whenever we have a trip planned. Sometimes they end up waiting more than an hour until I'm ready to start the car, but they simply can't help themselves: They're just *so excited* for our next family road trip!

I wrote this book because I know many parents don't feel the same. Some folks feel nervous about traffic or detours; others worry about backseat bickering. While the games within this book can't fix potholes or remedy rush hour, they *can* make the entire trip more fun for everyone.

When I was little, my parents, siblings and I played car games endlessly. My husband and I are doing the same with our girls. And I hope they'll look fondly back on these days—and maybe even play the same games with their own kids in the future.

You've reached the end of this book, but it's not the end of the road! You can return to these activities time and again. I'm so honored I get to play a small part in your family's journey.

Travel well,
xo Catherine

Your Next Steps

You might have reached this page and wondered, *Where to next?*

The truth is, I'd love to be part of your next adventure!

Here's how.

- Head over to my family travel blog, ToAndFroFam.com. You'll find recommendations for kid-friendly destinations, ideas for fun travel activities, travel hacks, tips on how to keep your kiddos happy en route, and even road trip-specific activities!

- Join the To & Fro Fam community. You can sign up for my newsletter that shares a must-know travel tip every week or join the conversation on Instagram, Facebook and Pinterest. (Look for @ToAndFroFam).

- Download a bunch of freebies for family travel, from an art museum scavenger hunt to family travel conversation starters. Find them all in one place at ToAndFroFam.com/ freebies.

- Read my other book, *Virtual Travel Activities for Kids* (on Amazon). In it, you'll find a year's worth of fun activities that help your littles learn about the world.

- Sign up for one of my workshops or courses! Find the latest, including how to rock your next road trip, at http://toandfrofam.com/ courses.

Index

Numbers

Out the window

Index

Printable

Teamwork

Word games

Index

About the Author

Catherine Ryan Gregory is a writer, travel-lover and author of *Virtual Travel Activities for Kids*. Her work has appeared in *Parents, Cosmopolitan, Women's Health, Marie Claire, Glamour* and *Self,* as well as many online outlets. She shares kid-friendly destinations and family travel hacks at ToAndFroFam.com. When she isn't traveling the world, she lives with her husband, two daughters and two rescue dogs outside Portland, Oregon.

Website: ToAndFroFam.com
Instagram: @ToAndFroFam
Pinterest: @ToFroFam
Facebook: Facebook.com/ToAndFroFam

Can You Help?

First off, thank you for reading Road Trip Games &
Activities for Kids! Next, I want to make my next
book and future editions of this one even better.

That's why I'd so appreciate your leaving an honest
review of the book online—where you bought it or
on a book-lover's platform like Goodreads.

Could you share your feedback?

Thank you!!
—Catherine

Made in United States
North Haven, CT
12 April 2022

18176363R00085